MANY THINGS INSPIRED MY WORKS, BUT NOTHING INSPIRED ME MORE
THAN THE PEOPLE THAT LIVE AND WORK IN THE SPACES I CREATE.
I STRIVE TO UNDERSTAND THEIR ASPIRATION TO REALIZE THEIR DREAM,
FOR THEY'RE THE FUEL THAT FIRES MY IMAGINATION

Hendra Hadiprana

THE AESTHETIC JOURNEY OF

HADIPRANA

Publishers of Architecture, Art, and Design
Gordon Goff: Publisher

www.oroeditions.com
info@oroeditions.com

Published by ORO Editions

Graphic Design: LeBoYe
Text: Diana Darling
Project Coordinator: Kirby Anderson

10 9 8 7 6 5 4 3 2 1 First Edition

Library of Congress data available upon request. World Rights: Available

ISBN: 978-1-9407438-7-5

Color Separations and Printing: ORO Group Ltd.
Printed in China.

International Distribution: www.oroeditions.com/distribution

ORO Editions makes a continuous effort to minimize the overall carbon
footprint of its publications. As part of this goal, ORO Editions, in
association with Global ReLeaf, arranges to plant trees to replace those
used in the manufacturing of the paper produced for its books. Global
ReLeaf is an international campaign run by American Forests, one of the
world's oldest nonprofit conservation organizations. Global ReLeaf is
American Forests' education and action program that helps individuals,
organizations, agencies, and corporations improve the local and global
environment by planting and caring for trees.

THE AESTHETIC JOURNEY OF
HADIPRANA

PHOTOGRAPHY BY LINDUNG SOEMARHADI

TEXT BY DIANA DARLING

ORO
EDITIONS

FOREWORD

This book is an invitation to enter the sumptuous world of Hadiprana, an Indonesian design firm, and to savor with the eyes, to taste with the imagination. It is unapologetically a picture book — that is, its information is primarily visual and immediately accessible. It does not state Hadiprana's design theories but, rather, reveals them in a guided presentation. It does this through a series of thematically grouped images that explore the intangible realm of feelings that inspire the design and that are produced in the viewer and the inhabitant.

The images are taken from ten recent projects by Hadiprana. Many of these projects include not only the architecture but also the interior design, the artwork, the landscaping, and specially created lighting.

The Introduction gives some background on the vast, beautiful archipelago that is Indonesia. It considers the cultural milieu in which the buildings were born and which they serve. It also contemplates the realm of hospitality as expressed in luxury architecture, whether resorts or private residences, from which these images are taken, particularly on the fabled island of Bali. The short chapter texts contemplate principal qualities that inspire and guide the Hadiprana design process.

We invite you to enjoy this book in a mood of repose and fantasy, and hope it will encourage more exploration of this prestigious design firm — and for those who do not yet know Indonesia, perhaps even a visit to this extraordinary country.

INTRODUCTION

To dwell therein like a king — that is the promise of the design of Hadiprana. In the images collected here, the reader will see glimpses of resorts, villas, and private residences designed by Hadiprana. All are designed for luxury hospitality. The inspiration for these comes from the palatial architecture of the former rulers of Indonesia, the vast equatorial archipelago between China and Australia. Indonesia has hundreds of distinct cultures, but the predominant one is that of Java, whose civilization has for centuries been supported by the fertility of its volcanic soils. The courts were powerful and much concerned with prestige.

The power of Javanese kings, though curtailed today through democracy, is legible in their *keraton* — the palaces that form the heart of classical royal towns such as Surakarta and Yogyakarta. The *keraton* is spread over a very large piece of land, surrounded by concentric walls. Grand gates lead through courtyard after courtyard, ever closer to the sacred center, which is adorned with symbols of pure stillness such as ponds and secret meditation pools.

Hadiprana finds inspiration from Indonesia's rich heritage, particularly from the *keraton*. The demands on modern luxury architecture are considerable. Villas and private residences designed by Hadiprana have generous spaces for receiving, entertaining, and accommodating guests. The owner finds seclusion and a connection with nature in his private quarters. In an up-scale resort, the designer faces the dilemma of providing many people with privacy and the experience of being at the center of the resort's attention. They must be welcomed, fed, bathed, and ushered to bed, all in a royal manner. They must be entertained and protected, for their leisure must not be disturbed by intrusion from the chaotic world they leave at the gate.

All this requires not only engineering but also ingenuity, a certain magic that can be achieved only by expert and sensitive design. In the images that follow, the reader will see the exercise of many design solutions to create a feeling of grandeur, of connectedness with nature and heritage, of intimacy with detail. The designers of Hadiprana employ the principles of progression of space, a mastery of focus, and the use of rhythm to create richness, all held in an elegant balance through symmetry around an axis. The result is harmony — both in the architecture and between the dweller and the built environment. Thus a dwelling suitable for a king. This is the art of Hadiprana.

ROMANCE is a quality of experience elevated from the ordinary. It arises from desire, a longing for beauty and for a world where all is gentle and noble. It evokes a realm of memory, an ancestral magical dream. Architecture inspires romance when it transcends the expectations of function and raises us to a higher dimension of being. The designer employs scale to create grandeur, and our heart expands with the space. Romance in architecture extends to the natural surroundings and incorporates them, weaving into the built space the land and the sky. It celebrates noble materials with the ingenuity of artisanship and the intimacy of detail.

HERITAGE is the human memory of creative accomplishment infused with spiritual intelligence. It is a way of doing things that is refined by time and the common experience of a society. It is an evolution of expertise tempered by social morality, to become the wisdom of a people and a way of teaching it to future generations.

As human beings, we respond to elements of heritage in architecture. It triggers a deep collective memory and brings us closer to a place. Through design, in the structure of space and use of materials, a place is infused with meaning. Details whisper a long forgotten story and stir the heart.

It is not only what pleases the eye. We crave a connection with our roots, with history, vernacular form, and the culture that connects us to our past and to each other.

NATURE is the source of our knowledge of
structure. Its mathematical beauty is revealed in
the golden mean and the Fibonacci series. In nature
we see the rules of balance and perceive the logic
of engineering, and can see symmetry and the excellence
of proportion. Our sense of beauty is formed by
the structural truth in nature.

Hadiprana consults nature for inspiration and seeks
to preserve our connection to nature. A building site
comprises not only the land on which a building sits
but also its environment, including views of the sea,
hills, rice fields, and distant sky. Water, sunlight, and
breezes are all elements for the designer to consider
and employ, so that we stand in the center, connected
to our natural surroundings.

The true balance of beauty is to be found in nature,
an ever-changing source of the grandeur that inspires the spirit.

ARTISANSHIP arises with the mastery of materials. It implies the exceptional. It entails a high level of dexterity, and a deep understanding of the nature of its subject materials — an ability to transform visions into objects, using the knowledge and processes of the guild or community of a particular art.

Artisanship serves the mythic memory of a society and keeps its truth fresh. Design employs artisanship to elevate the value of an object with the impact of the human hand and collective wisdom. Artisanship imbues an object with dignity, and therefore also the space it occupies.

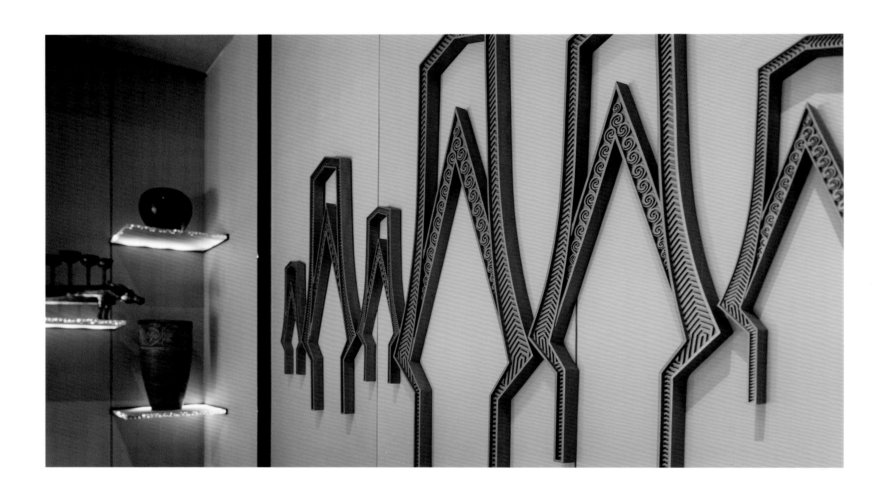

Artisanship brings us close to an object. It creates intimacy.
The details are not the design. They are story elements that make
the design.

RHYTHM is order in all organic movement, from the breath and the heartbeat to the structure of song. We seek rhythm in logic and the progression of ideas. In architecture, rhythm is the ordering of space and movement from one space to the next. It moves in procession from the cacophony of the exterior world to the calm inner center. Rhythm employs repetition to create pattern. In the community, it is the chant in enchantment and incantation. Rhythm is also expressed in layers, moving through levels of meaning and accumulating strength as we move from one space to the next.

PROCESSION is vitality in the coherent ordering of space. There is progression from the exterior toward the center. But because the center is sacred, it must be achieved gradually, just as the initiate moves through stages of knowledge.

In the *keraton* idiom evoked by the architecture of Hadiprana, we leave the world behind and enter a palatial world, the grand reception space, and then approach the realm of the social — the courtyard, the banquet room for invited guests — to privacy and finally to the intimate: the study, the bathing space, the place for prayer, for love, for sleep.

There is a feeling of continual visual and spatial discovery. To move through the space is to encounter its richness within the geometry.

REPETITION expressed rhythmically is pattern,
an element of ornamentation. This is the exuberant and
fanciful aspect of the natural world, of Creation celebrating
its brilliance: think of the pattern on the scales of a serpent.
Repetition brings stability and strength: think of the
serpent's ribs, or of the pillars of a mansion's veranda.

Repetition is an element of the screen. It allows our eye
to first savor the pattern and sense its stability, and then
to acknowledge the realm beyond it. And repetition is an
expression of the collective, a signal of a gathering place
where people come together.

When we experience the rhythm of repetition, we find repose in its vitality.

LAYER is sequence. A space is comprised of layers
of meaning, each contributing to the visual texture.
One element opens to another and leads our eye to
different aspects of function and interest. Framing changes
with movement may be an element of interest on its own.
A screen or a doorway opens and invites; a window brings
an exchange between interior and exterior.

Layer creates the atmosphere of a space and tells a story.
It is the quality of context and connection, which make up
a multi-dimensional space and give a sense of abundance.

A sequence of layers creates procession through an interplay of solid and void, at each stage bringing us closer to the center and the self.

ELEGANCE is what distinguishes good architectural design from merely construction. It is the charisma of a place, the magnetism that draws us in and makes us happy to have arrived there. It is more than the appearance of a space; it has a specific energy and emotional color created by the nature of the materials and the way they are used. Elegance is precision in the choice and treatment of materials, setting them in play through pattern and craftsmanship. It is establishing focus in a room and providing balance around a center. Elegance creates a feeling of being harmonious with the world.

CHARACTER is the materiality of a place, the choice of materials and how they are worked to produce texture, pattern, and the play of forms and surfaces. A grid may be complemented by the soft, round forms of upholstery, or bathe a space in a pattern of shadows. A wall of stone becomes a geometrical composition. A combination of different screens tells a more complex story about a view.

Materials take on a distinctive textural character for being worked into patterns and juxtaposed to other materials in a manner that surprises us and makes us think about them in a fresh way.

A space arrests us in the feel of texture and pattern, in the experience of light and space in a particular room, and asks us to linger there.

ACCENTUATION is a way of working with
focus. It may be accomplished with placement, with
framing or isolation, with contrast, or with color or light.
An accented object acts on the space around it, pulls it in,
and creates a field of attention. The designer draws our
attention to something because of its function or simply
because of its beauty.

At Hadiprana, the design choice is always to provide
a point of focus rather than to simply clutter all four walls
with decoration. We will always find a point of focus for
the eye as we move about the space.

Composition controls degrees of prominence and permits the making of a statement — which may be solemn, sensual, instructive, or simply joyful.

P O I S E in architecture is an ineffable quality
of grace and balance. It is the bounty of a multitude
of harmonious elements in space, composed in a living
whole. Whether the idiom is traditional, eclectic, or
contemporary, Hadiprana design always provides an axis
that affords symmetry and creates balance in spaces from
grand to intimate.

The axis may be anything from a wall, an object,
an ornamental source of light, to a pool of water. It may
be vertical or horizontal. It is the invisible organizational
principle that gives a space coherence and integrity,
and puts us at ease.

To find balance in everything in order to please our primary instinct. The balance is a dynamic one, inviting us to move amongst its elements in discovery.

Built forms evolve and revolve through eras, but the human notion of space and time
never evolves far from comfort, the perception of luxury, and connectivity to where it belongs.
Through Romance, Rhythm, and Elegance, Hadiprana establishes its roots:
its guidance for an endless journey of aesthetic exploration.

The Hadiprana design team

Our highest gratitudes

to our founder: Hendra Hadiprana, for his vision and guidance,

to our clients, colleagues, and partners:
Sari and Jani Winata, Ani Wati and Fenza Sofyan,
Anie and Hashim Djojohadikusumo, Linda and Garibaldi Thohir,
Lilik Oetama, Soetjipto Nagaria, Soegianto Nagaria, Herman Nagaria,
Elly and Thomas Halim, Edwin Halim, Benyamin Syarif,
Muljadi Budiman, Agung Budiman, Feroline Kurniawan,
Rosano Barack, Boyke Gozali, Ferdinand Gumanti, and Helen Gumanti,
for their generous contributions,

and to our team, for the hardwork.

Mira Hadiprana

CONTENT CREATOR & EDITOR Faried Masdoeki. Afwina Kamal. Himawan Sutanto. Meita Tristida Arethusa | PHOTOGRAPHER Lindung Soemarhadi | TEXT Diana Darling | GRAPHIC DESIGNER LeBoYe | PROJECT COORDINATOR Meita Tristida Arethusa. Eko Warsito | STYLIST Ami Utami. Afwina Kamal. Sammy Hendramianto. Shinta Meirina Hapsari. Dwi Astuti Kusumaningrum. Ika Handayani. Puriyanti Ismail. Twiceastian Fastiary Nugroho. Lorina Lumombo. Trivesti Laksmi Paramitha. Revinna Therasiana. Boy Ariewibowo. Arianto Suryowibowo. Himawan Sutanto. Meita Tristida Arethusa. I Gusti Ayu Surya Dewi. Ketut Suartana. Wawan Wigianto. I Made Yudi Hariyawan. Didik Anas Ahmadi | FUNDRAISING Ami Utami. Ika Marthawati. Mesalina. Sastyhartanti. Arizka Sibpryani. Ika Handayani.

LIST OF IMAGES

ANVAYA BEACH RESORT

The Anvaya is one of the premium members of Santika Indonesia Hotels & Resorts. Located in the center of Kuta, Bali, the Anvaya Beach Resort benefits from its own private sandy beach and is equipped with a wide range of features and amenities. The ambience of the Anvaya architecture is inspired by Bali's rich cultural history, from the ancient times of the Bali Aga to Hindu Bali and Modern Bali.

Finalist for REKA International Design Award 2017
Nominee for HDII Award 2017
Sands Restaurant
    2nd Runner Up for Best Mediterranean Restaurant
Best Restaurant Bar & Cafe
    Now Bali Magazine Awards 2017

Architecture: Hadiprana
Interior: Hadiprana
Special Lighting: Hadiprana
Landscape: Intaran Design Inc.
Artwork: Hadiprana & Intaran Design Inc.

GRAND CAFE AT GRAND HYATT JAKARTA

Grand Café has been serving guests since the Grand Hyatt Jakarta first opened its door in July 1991. After almost 30 years, this cafe is in need of a younger, fresher look. Hirsch Bedner Associates was in charge of the renovation. Completing the new face, Hadiprana is in charge of the artworks and décor. Our intention is to give a local touch to the new café, a taste of Indonesia, to keep the identity of Jakarta's landmark Grand Hyatt.

Interior: Hirsch Bedner Associates
Special Lighting: Illuminate Lighting & Design
Artwork: Hadiprana

KERATON AT THE PLAZA

Urban residences stay in the center of Jakarta where functionality is a priority. Thus, a touch of artisanship is important to indulge souls into the dynamic of Indonesia's local beauty, to remind them where the city belongs. Hadiprana was responsible for setting and creating the artworks inspired by the richness of the keraton, Indonesia's traditional palace.

Interior: Burega Farnel
Special Lighting: Hadi Komara & Associates
Artwork: Hadiprana

MOVENPICK RESORT AND SPA

This is a 5-star family resort less than five minutes' walk from Jimbaran Beach, South Bali. The heart of this resort is the massive attraction dedicated for families in particular. Guests can swim in a generously sized lap pool, or relax at a fun pool integrated with hammocks, while kids are having fun in the pirate-themed Meera Kids Club. This resort offers casual luxury ambience inspired by Balinese seaside villages.

Finalist for REKA International Design Award 2017
Nominee for HDII Award 2017
Movenpick Cafe
    2nd Runner Up Best Cafe,
    Best Restaurant Bar & Cafe - Now Bali Magazine
    Award 2017

Architecture: Cadiz International & Hadiprana
Interior: Hadiprana, bench at lobby by Alvin
Special Lighting: Litac
Landscape: Salad Dressing
Artwork: Hadiprana

ROYAL TULIP GUNUNG GEULIS RESORT GOLF

To frame nature is the main soul of this project. Located inside a golf course at Ciawi, Bogor, this resort is surrounded by majestic landscape and unobstructed views of the mountain. It is a perfect destination for alternative incentive venues, weekend family escapade, or even weddings. The building itself is toned in a modern and functional way.

Winner of Commercial Design Award 2016 - Style & Decor Magazine
Winner of HDII Award 2017
Continent Winner of World Luxury Hotel Award 2017

Architecture: Hadiprana
Interior: Hadiprana
Special Lighting: Hadiprana
Landscape: Hadiprana
Artwork: Hadiprana

RUMAH LUWIH

'The house for kings' is the main concept of the design. Rumah Luwih is a beachfront boutique resort with limited room numbers but complemented by exquisite facilities and amenities. The design is inspired by colonial Indonesian mansions. The challenge is to find a balance: to implement the concept of grandeur while maintaining the highest respect for the locality of Bali.

Nominee for Commercial Design Award 2016 - Style & Decor Magazine
Nominee for HDII Award 2017

Architecture: Hadiprana
Interior: Hadiprana
Special Lighting: Hadiprana
Landscape: Hadiprana
Artwork: Hadiprana

CLIFF VILLA IN BALI

Situated on the hilly side of southern Bali, facing the ocean, this holiday villa offers beautiful views all day long. To create the feeling of contemporary Bali, it uses mostly natural materials which are articulated in a modern way. Though it has to meet practicality values, this villa manages to create a connection between inside (human) and outside (nature).

Architecture: Hadiprana
Interior: Hadiprana
Special Lighting: Hadiprana
Landscape: Hadiprana
Artwork: Hadiprana

Page 2, 3, 12, 13, 60, 61, 72, 73, 110 left bottom, 110 right bottom, 111 left top, 130 left top, 130 right bottom, 163, 187, 199 left top, 218, 220 left bottom, 220 right bottom, 221 left top, 221 right top, 226, 230, 231

HILL RESIDENCE IN BALI

The owner's love for Indonesian culture and heritage is what shaped the design of this house. Hadiprana was responsible for the design of the interior and artworks, a means to answer the built architecture with the richness of Indonesia's sense of beauty.

Winner of HDII Award 2014

Architecture: PT Canggah Wang (Cheong Yew Kuan)
Interior: Hadiprana
Special Lighting: Hadi Komara & Associates
Landscape: PT Bukit Kembar Permai
Artwork: Hadiprana

Page 52, 114, 118, 139

RESIDENCE AT MENTENG

This renovation and extension project challenged one's principle of luxury hospitality by the obligation to preserve the original colonial façade. Located in the prestigious neighborhood of Menteng, Jakarta, there was no negotiation in the duty to create a grand atmosphere. The building has to convey a feeling of establishment and formality but at once accommodating the new generation's perception of comfort.

Architecture: Hadiprana
Interior: Hadiprana
Special Lighting: Hadiprana
Landscape: Hadiprana
Artwork: Hadiprana

Page 44 left top, 45 left top, 46, 76, 77, 86 right bottom, 104, 125, 129, 131 left top, 150 right top, 151 right bottom, 160, 171, 173, 174, 175, 177, 179 left bottom, 198 right bottom, 207, 208, 214, 220 left top, 224

SEASIDE HOUSE IN BALI

Sequences were created to take occupants from the outside world (gate) to a magnificent view of the sunset on the sea. Along this passage are functional spaces, which then create an intense connection between indoors and nature. Instead of a living room, it is the sequence of courtyards that becomes the heart of the house. Yet, the journey of the passage ends with the two most functional spaces of a house: living room and dining room.

Architecture: Hadiprana
Interior: Hadiprana
Special Lighting: Hadiprana
Landscape: Hadiprana
Artwork: Hadiprana & Sunaryo

Page 4, 5, 6, 7, 8, 9, 14, 15, 37, 40, 41, 43, 45 right top, 53, 54, 55, 59, 64 left bottom, 65 left top, 65 left bottom, 70, 86 right top, 87, left bottom, 96, 97, 108, 111 left bottom, 116, 130 right top, 150 right bottom, 152, 153, 178 right bottom, 179 right top, 184, 185, 199 right top, 219

HEARTFELT GRATITUDE TO

Fasetti